Inside This Dress

Dakima Maria

Inside This Dress

God Turned My Pain Into Rose Petals

XULON PRESS

Xulon Press
2301 Lucien Way #415
Maitland, FL 32751
407.339.4217
www.xulonpress.com

© 2018 by Dakima Maria

All rights reserved solely by the author. The author guarantees all contents are original and do not infringe upon the legal rights of any other person or work. No part of this book may be reproduced in any form without the permission of the author. The views expressed in this book are not necessarily those of the publisher.

Unless otherwise indicated, Scripture quotations taken from the New King James Version (NKJV). Copyright © 1982 by Thomas Nelson, Inc. Used by permission. All rights reserved.

Printed in the United States of America.

ISBN-13: 978-1-54562-367-1

Table of Contents

Introduction ix
Foreword xv

One: Exquisite Array with Frayed Seams. 1
Two: Delicate Array With Torn Layers 9
Three: Bedazzled Vestments with Interwoven Stratums 19
Four: Celebratory Array with Ruffled Fibers. 27
Five: Elaborate Masquerades with Closures 39
Six: Intricate Gear Ready for Tussle .47
Seven: Excessive Truss Wrapped Around my Frock 59
Eight: My Children's Point of View 63
Nine: Exaggerated Array with Exclusive Remnants 71
Ten: Elegant Array with Rectified Ridges 75

Introduction

My beautiful readers, as you glance over the chapters of my life, I hope that you can reflect on your own. We have all experienced heartaches and happiness at some point in our lives.

Writing this book freed me from the trauma of my past and created an opportunity for me to live my best life. Maybe you've gone through some things that you've never shared with others that may have somehow created insecurities within yourself. Hopefully, this book will help you recognize how to move forward with your best life.

During this season in my life, I am pursuing my career as a licensed cosmetologist, and attending college to obtain my Bachelor of Fine Arts degree in fashion design. I am passionate about the beauty industry. I decided to get creative and have fun while writing my book. Each chapter represents a type of dress, with different seams, for every occasion in my life.

Take a glance over your own life and leap in a healthier mindset of self-awareness. Find the ability to build stronger determination from within yourself. Contemplate and create authentic confidence that cannot be swayed.

Eliminating distractions are crucial for me, I am easily distracted. I am learning how to create a plan and carry it out. When I don't plan I am mentally scattered all over the place.

I am not looking for sympathy or a hand out because of my story. I am simply encouraging readers to know that if I can overcome homelessness, raise five children as a single mom, and continue to strive for my best future, so can you!

To everyone who has seen me strive and contributed in any way—from the homes opened up to us to the Christmas gifts sent from all over the world. To the family who took my boys every summer to show them a different environment. To those who helped get my children through sports and into college. To everyone who took me under your wings and taught me how to soar. To all my family and friends, thank you for sharing your kindness it is greatly appreciated.

Dakima Hicks is my auntie. She is definitely a part of the village that helped raised me into the woman I am today. She's been a mentor, a motivator, a disciplinarian, and sort of like a therapist. My aunt has always instilled in me the importance of simply being me. Even though it sounds simple, it's hard for many people like myself to achieve. She would tell me to do things based on what I wanted to do. She constantly expressed that to me with encouraging words, so you could also say she was like my coach. I am very proud of her. She has come so far in life and God has much more in store for her. My aunt has not only talked the talk but she has displayed through action how to be a woman of faith. Being courageous and following God's will is how she got to where she is today. I'm excited to see where she goes in life, because I know without a shadow of a doubt, that it's going to be a place bigger than any of us can even imagine.

Deaunai Montgomery, loving niece

Dakima's story is one not to be missed for those seeking inspiration. Her life journey is captivating and ever so real for many women and single moms. During challenge after challenge and setback after setback, Dakima's faith and optimistic spirit remained unwavering. You'll find yourself cheering her on as you read each page! Dakima reminds us of the many peaks and valleys in life, while giving messages of encouragement and the power of hope through all of them.

Sally Schoen

When I think of Dakima Hicks, I think of a strong and resilient woman. I often think I could never do what she does. I am amazed that despite some the things that she has gone through, she still shines like a star.

I can remember being late to church and seeing her on the pew with her children dressed and on time. I would say to myself, "I have got to do better." She set an example for me and from then on, I was always intrigued by her personality and sweet kids. Her friendliness was something that really stuck with me. She always kept a smile through it all.

She is brave and fearless, willing to go for what she wants even if it goes against popular opinion. Her kids are blessed to have a mom who will do what it takes to make sure they are successful. I know it may have been a hard road, but look at how far she's come. Here she is writing a book. Who wouldn't want to support and encourage a woman who never quits.

Timmi

My big sister Dakima was always brave and a leader. She was a person who had faith and God always showed up. I have always joked that I felt like God heard her prayers and not mine. Every time God sent her on a journey, she went. When people told her not to, she still went. We went all the way to New York, with no money, and God showed up, enabling my sister to accomplish her mission. We had shelter and food! My sister is a role model to so many, including me. I thank God for allowing her to share her story with you all.

Dakima you touched so many lives, you are truly a blessing to me. I love you.

Tisha

I've had the pleasure of engaging on many levels with a vast number of professionals and students throughout my teaching career and mentoring journey. Dakima Hicks is one of the few who made a lasting impression on me. Dakima and I first met at Euphoria Institute of Beauty and Science in her pursuit of a career in cosmetology. I recall receiving Dakima into my class on day one of her academic journey. Right away she displayed her commitment and dedication to her chosen profession. We quickly developed a connection and as the days went on, I would be privileged enough to learn of Dakima's life testimony. Her story of victory and triumph in the face of trials, road blocks, neglect, and persecution would explain why today she is so convicted in her pursuit of happiness at all cost for her and her beautiful children. The example of strength and perseverance that she continues to set for all of those who encounter her organic personality and her "I can do ALL things through Christ that strengthens me" attitude continue to wow me. Who would have thought that on the day Dakima and I met, we would later exchange our life lessons and embark on a beautiful exchange of love, sisterhood, and even family. I am so proud of the woman she has become. Dakima will move forward to become a pillar of wisdom and strength in her community and a true light to this world.

Keita Williams

Foreword

I am the proud mother of the beautiful, intelligent, talented, faithful, entrepreneur, and new author *Dakima Maria Hicks*. I am sure you will love this inspiring book. It will give you amazing hope, encouragement, and strength to move forward. Dakima, is a God fearing woman. She loves God, her children, family and friends. Dakima has never been fake or phony, in any shape, form, or fashion. When she was growing up, I told her to speak her mind and that is exactly what she will do today.

Dakima and her sister were in my brother's wedding when they were about 5 and 7 years old. Their uncle purchased their dresses, socks, and everything they needed to be the flower girls. Dakima was a fashion model and designer at a very young age. While at the wedding reception, she pulled her dress down off her shoulders and modeled for everyone.

In middle school and high school, Dakima was always getting into some type of trouble, and I would receive a call asking me to come pick her up. She wasn't a bad person, she just wanted attention and I wasn't giving it to her. She wanted me home more spending time with her and her siblings, and I wasn't. I was married, but raising my three children alone. Their father was never home, and when he was, he was abusive. I worked three jobs to make ends meet.

Dakima's older brother would tell the girls at school who picked on him, *"I am gonna tell my sister."* Dakima was known as a fighter, and they didn't want to get into it with her.

Praise God! Dakima, grew up and matured! She loves to praise and worship her Savior, Jesus Christ. She is truly an entrepreneur. She owned a candy shop. She's a fashion designer, both designing and making the clothing. She's a hairstylist, a makeup artist, and a gorgeous mother of five beautiful children! She raised the five children on her own after her divorce from their father. I am so proud of her and my grandchildren. She drove herself and five children to Las Vegas to start a new chapter in her life. God blessed her with a home and furnished it. Each time she moved, the house got bigger and better!

She's always calling me with a testimony of God's provision. It is truly amazing to hear my daughter's faith and the excitement in her voice as she talks about the love she has for God and how she trusts Him! Dakima has shared so many awesome testimonies and miracles of how God has blessed her over and over and over again.

Yes, Dakima loves the Lord! Yes, she allows the Lord to lead her! Yes, Jesus Christ is her provider! However, she has had times in her life when she had to cry, when she didn't hear God's voice, and she didn't know which way to go. As you will see, through all her tears, all her questions, and all her waiting, God always came through right on time.

Ruth J. Webb, Dakima's mother

Chapter One

Exquisite Array with Frayed Seams

On July 27, 1975, an attractive, fair-skinned little girl with dark, straight hair, big brown eyes, and a gorgeous smile was born at Sinai Grace Hospital in Detroit Michigan. Her parents named her Dakima. That little girl was me. I was born to Ruth and Dillard Collier III, newlyweds, who married on June 30, 1975, just about a month before I was born. Both of my parents came from large families. My maternal and paternal grandmothers were very active in my life. I didn't know either one of my grandfathers. My aunts and uncles Pitched in where they could as I was growing up. I have two siblings, an older brother and a younger sister. We grew up like military kids except my parents weren't in the military. We transitioned to multiple locations and schools around the city. Our stability was altered on many occasions.

As a young girl, my mom was leaving out for work, I ran behind her. I reached my arms out toward her as she was shutting the door. My fingertip got caught in the door and was sliced off! My mom rushed me to the nearest hospital. The doctor tried to replace my finger but once he stitched my fingertip back on, my hand turned blue because of the lack of circulation. The doctor immediately removed the fingertip and bandaged it.

Over time my fingertip grew back deformed. I was teased about it in school. Classmates told me that it looked like a male's anatomy or an apple when I wore fingernail polish. I was ashamed to the point of hiding my hand. Now, I am so thankful for my finger, because it's a part of me that makes me so special. Being left handed and having a pre-auricular sinus, which is basically a pre-made piercing at birth where the face and ear cartilage meet, also makes me unique.

Growing up we lived in a beautifully decorated three-bedroom bungalow. Me and my sister shared rooms. My brother had his own room. My dad worked at Ford Motor Company in Dearborn, MI. My mom worked at Ross Roy, Bloomfield Hills, MI.

One day, my dad came home from work in a good mood. He threw money on the floor, and it scattered everywhere. My eyes got so big, my heart was overjoyed, and I immediately started reaching for the money. He told us to pick up whatever we wanted, so my sister and I picked up a five-dollar bill. My brother picked up a fifty-dollar bill. I tried changing mine after picking up a small bill, but my dad said, "Put it back." My mom and dad took us to the store so that we could use the money to buy ourselves some candy. We were so excited.

Although, I was extremely young at the time, those were my best childhood memories, until my dad was intoxicated beyond his limits and became very aggressive, angry, and abusive. I was afraid of him. I tried to get away from him or pretend to be happy around him.

My parent's relationship baffled me. When my dad was home, he slept with my mom, beat her, and left for multiple days at a time. Other times he brought gifts home and hung out with us for the night. We didn't know what to expect when he left returned home. Can you imagine the unpredictable feeling I must have felt as a little girl?

The dysfunction inside my home was detrimental for me. The pain and agony from my youth spilled over into my adolescence and extended into my adulthood. As I sit here and write with tears flowing in remembrance of the violence. Other horrific incidents happened during my childhood.

My dad came home from work, livid. He approached my mom with force and beat her brutally with consistent punches to the face. Her face swelled and blood was dripping off. My mom kept asking us to call the police, but my dad told me not to move. So, I stood in the corner and did not budge. Standing there unable to scream for help, watching my dad abuse my mom, was so painful. I was most disappointed that my mom didn't press any charges, once the police arrived.

One time, my mom went running down the street with her finger dangling off her hand in search of someone to help her. I couldn't say anything or follow her. Shortly after she left the house, I heard sirens coming towards our street. It was the EMS picking up my mom. She came home with stitches and a bandage. We went on with life like nothing ever happened.

Another time I was in the car with my family. Something must have happened to change the atmosphere. My dad made a quick turn toward the bridge. My sister was sitting on my mom's lap in the front seat. My mom jumped out of the car with her arms tightly wrapped around my sister. Me and my brother was in the back seat, I was scared. My dad stopped the car and told my mom to get back in or he was going to drive off the bridge with us in the car. She and my sister got back in the car, and once again, we went home as if nothing ever happened.

After walking home from a long day of school, my mom called to me from upstairs, "Your dad has a gun and won't allow me to come down. Go to your room." I heard him say, "Shut-up! I will blow your brains out, kill the kids, and then kill myself. Shut-up." Immediately, I went into my room and stayed there like a turtle in his shell. It wasn't until later that evening that my mom came down, and again life went on.

There were times that my dad took us with him when he and mom argued. We visited the mistress who was in his life during that time. His behaviors were the same with them as my mom. Except, we did more activities such as went to the park, movies, and dinner.

A woman was pregnant by my dad. Somehow, she had a conversation with my mom. The woman came to our house, she and my mom appeared to be plotting something against my dad. It backfired. I was sitting on the sofa in the living room when my dad walked through the door. He looked at them both and asked what was going on. He walked around cussing, saying I have something for you both. He went into the kitchen, took out a hammer. He beat their feet with a hammer and used his fist everywhere else. The lady lost her baby.

We moved away again and went back and forth at what seemed like about hundred times or more. During several episodes, my dad hid me from my mom. He took me to his mother's home, Chrissy Collier. Who we have in loving memories. The phone rang, it was my mom. Grandma Chrissy told me that I would get spanked if I said anything. She tried to compensate me by taking me shopping, out to eat, or polishing my nails. Although I loved my grandma, I was so hurt when she participated in deceiving my mom. It was hard for me to sleep at night. I used to sit by the corner of her bed and cry my eyes out. One day, her toes caught my attention. I kept thinking how ghastly her toes looked. Guess whose toes look just like hers— mine.

By the time I was seven years old, my dad's youngest brother Robert Collier, had been molesting me for some time. When I went to grandma Chrissy's house, Robert took me into the basement so that he could touch my private area and put his tongue down my throat. I tensed up every time I saw his face. I experienced so many different emotions. He scared me into not sharing his behavior with my parents.

I was fed up with his behavior. I needed someone to help me. An after school special came on television with a little girl experiencing something very similar. I couldn't stop crying. I kept thinking I needed to tell my mom, but I didn't want to get in any trouble. I had an urge inside me to run into the kitchen and hug my mom, so I did. I was crying even harder. My mom asked me what was wrong. I asked her if I could tell her anything. She replied, "Yes." So, I told her all about what Robert was doing to me. She started crying along with me and asked me how long this had been happening.

My mom grabbed me by my hand and drove over to my grandmother's home immediately. When we arrived, my mom told my Robert never to touch me again or she would kill him. She was furious! I was never forced to go over there again. I often wish I'd told my mom much sooner after seeing her response.

At birth, I was given parents to raise me with love, protection, and provision. They couldn't possibly succeed in completing that task with so much physical, verbal, and mental abuse going on inside the home. They were literally trying to survive moment by moment.

As a child, I formed an opinion about my parents, their behaviors towards one another, my siblings, and me. My dad was overbearing, and my mom was passive aggressive. The home was so peaceful when my dad was away. I couldn't understand why my mom accepted so much abuse and neglect. I disagreed with what was going on, but I also knew that I couldn't pick or choose my parents.

I didn't realize how much my childhood affected me until I was in my thirties. So many times, I persecuted myself. I defended every mistake, and I made excuses for anything that wasn't a good decision. I was extremely insecure, very needy, and never felt good enough. The emptiness I felt was overwhelming, to the point of desiring to sleep my whole day away. I definitely needed change. But how could I change when I didn't understand what to change.

After researching women who were successful in the public eye, I gained a different perspective about life. I noticed that each of them had a significant story, with some degree of pain, and a push of determination. Harriet Tubman freed herself from slavery. When she returned to get her husband, he had already taken on another wife. She didn't stop there! She followed the North Star and freed so many others. Maya Angelou met a guy from South Africa. She moved to Africa for a short period of time, after returning to the states she wrote a book. They made mistakes, but they turned them into learning experiences. Which caused me to get creative, ambitious, and adventurous with my own life.

    I am even more determined to take a stand, make a difference, and share my story with the world, instead of being embarrassed about my past. My freedom comes from God; my happiness comes from within; and my successes or failures are generated by me. I don't look down on anyone who has hurt me. I choose to forgive everyone who has contributed to any of my pain or disappointments. I have also hurt others. While I might not have hurt them intentionally as long as I live it is bound to happen. I also forgive myself daily. I take full responsibility for my decisions. I believe that I was destined to have these different experiences to give me the courage that I have today. I am not afraid to walk in faith because at different points in my life, faith was all that I had.

Chapter Two

Delicate Array With Torn Layers

When I was seven years old, my mom received a call that my dad was taken into custody for attempted murder. We weren't living with my dad at the time. When we pulled up to the bungalow home, we saw that the windows and the door had been boarded up. As my mom, my sister, and I walked towards the house, I felt estranged because of what I heard when my mom got off the phone. I wondered what really occurred in the house and could that have been me, if I was there.

My mom opened the front door with me close by her side. When we walked into the house, I immediately noticed blood everywhere. It was splashed on the walls, and on the carpet in the living room. There were puddles of blood around the kitchen.

My mom explained to me that my dad and one of his brother's, Thomas Collier was at a night club with one of their friend's, Antonio Evers. They were highly intoxicated. Antonio left my dad, and uncle Thomas at the night club. When Antonio showed up at the bungalow, my dad and uncle Thomas jumped him. They burned him with an iron all over his body and left him to die. He was rushed to the hospital, and surprisingly he survived after losing so much blood.

My dad and uncle Thomas went to jail. My dad served time while he was on trial. My mom wanted to be there for my dad during this period of time. She reconciled their differences. Anything my dad needed, my mom was right there. If he needed her to file papers, send money to his account, or write a letter, she did it.

As we sat outside the courtroom on the first day of the trial, my dad's attorney told us that we couldn't have any contact with the victim or his family. It wasn't like this man was a stranger. He was close to our family, and we had to act like we didn't know him. I was more nervous about walking into the courtroom, than actually being in the courtroom. The fear of the unknown crept up on me.

It was hard to go into the courtroom to support my dad knowing he was guilty, though innocent until proven guilty. My mom dressed my sister and me in beautiful dresses and black dress shoes with ruffled white socks folded at the ankle. She had our hair pulled nice and smooth into two ponytails. She took us both by the hand, and we walked through the double doors of the courtroom.

As we walked into the courtroom, I was looking down at the floor with anxiety and fear of what was going to happen next arose inside me. We sat on the left side, the second row from the witness stand. We were asked to stand as the judge entered the room. Shortly after, I saw the security guard walking with my dad into the courtroom. He looked at me and smiled and I smiled back.

My dad was wearing an orange jumpsuit. His hair was slicked back into a ponytail, and he had cuffs around his ankles and his hands. The security guard removed the cuffs from around his ankle and walked my dad to the witness stand. As both lawyers questioned my dad, I visualized his answers. I was dismayed, yet thankful that it wasn't me on the witness stand. It severely affected my heart to observe my dad and his former friend testify against one another in court. I can't really remember what happened during the trial although, I sat in the courtroom during the case.

It came time for my dad to get arraigned. I can't completely remember that process, besides the time when the jury had to leave the courtroom to discuss the verdict. The exact same nervous feeling I had when I walked through the doors of the courtroom for the first time revisited me. I looked up at my mom, over at my sister, and wondered what was going to happen next.

Finally, the jury walked back into the courtroom. The judge asked for the verdict. My heart was beating so fast inside my chest, my legs started swinging, and my hands were so sweaty. As the verdict was read, I closed my eyes.

My dad was proven guilty on every count pertaining to his charges. I looked up at my mom and over at my sister; they both were crying. I started balling with tears that wouldn't stop falling down my face. As I was leaving the courtroom, I remember thinking that I would never see my dad again. I don't know what happened to my uncle Thomas.

My dad was given ten to fifteen years as his sentence. My mom hugged my sister and me and told us everything was going to be okay. Part of me was happy he was gone, and another part felt brokenhearted. I didn't understand how to express my emotions, communicate effectively, or eliminate the feelings of abandonment.

As a young child, going to visit my dad in prison was entirely devastating. We frequently drove long hours to get there, regardless if it was sunny, gloomy, or rainy. As my mom parked the car, we had to eat a snack before going inside. To enter the facility, we had to go through a metal detector. As we sat in the waiting area, my sister and I always wanted something from the vending machine. But we knew that our mom told us before we went in not to ask. The security guard came from behind these huge metal doors and yelled, "Collier," along with some identification numbers that represented my dad.

We sat in an area with lots of grass, picnic tables, and a small playground for children. Although it was devastating going to prison to see my dad, once I got inside, I ran around on the playground and played board games and card games. Sometimes our extended family visited my dad with us. When we went back to our hotel my siblings, cousins, and I had fun hanging out.

When I think about my interactions with my dad personally during those visits, I can't remember much happiness. I do remember my dad being aggressive, and emotional. For example, He would fuss at me and then cry about how much he loves me shortly after. I didn't understand why, until I had children of my own, and repeated that same cycle.

One tragic day, on our way home from visiting my father, my mother fell asleep at the wheel, and we were in a head on car collision. I came to sitting on the ground and wet from rain. I was 9 years old.

There was a reporter who repeatedly asked me, "Are you ok?" She then proceeded to ask me, "How old are you? How old is your sister? How old is your brother?" It happened to be one of the rare times that my brother went with us.

I looked around at my surroundings trying to figure out what was happening. When I saw my mom, I started to scream, my heart was broken, and I thought she was going to die. Her face was disfigured and swollen to the size of a basketball. She looked over at me and said, " God is with us and everything will be okay."

My mom was taken by helicopter to another hospital because her injuries were too severe for the closest hospital. She had a broken jaw, a broken nose, a busted knee-cap, and a busted tear duct.

My sister was also transported to another hospital by an ambulance with two broken hips and a broken leg. My brother had a broken arm and a busted chin. I broke my wrist and busted my eye.

My maternal uncle and grandma came to pick my brother and me up from the hospital. They took us to McDonald's before taking us to see my mom. When I arrived at the hospital, many family members were in the waiting area. My eyes scanned the room as I feared the unknown. I wondered what was going on as I overheard the adults talking about the doctors not thinking my mom was going to survive. They called the family in to prepare us for the worst. I immediately started praying, and I couldn't imagine being without both of my parents.

My mom was in the hospital for a month. During that time, my dad was allowed to visit her once, accompanied by an officer. When my mom was finally released, the doctors restricted her diet and activities and said she needed adequate rest.

My sister was in the hospital for a month as well, she came home shortly after my mom. She was in a wheelchair, and the doctor's told her that she would never walk again. We were in the kitchen one day, and my sister said, "I will walk again." She got up out of the wheelchair and put one foot in front of the other until she could balance herself. She has been walking ever since.

My brother and I were the least injured. I had to learn how to write with my right hand for approximately six to eight weeks. It was very challenging for me in the beginning, until I kept practicing.

After a while, everything seemed to start falling back into place. My mom went back to work, and my siblings and I returned to school shortly after her return home from the hospital. My mom worked two jobs and went to school full-time. I never saw her relax, enjoy herself, or get away alone. She was always trying to figure out how to pay the bills.

One day, we were all at home together, which was very unusual due to my mom's schedule. I went into the kitchen, opened the cabinets, and closed them back with disgust written all over my face. I was saddened because we didn't have any food. Not even basic items like, peanut butter and jelly, crackers, rice, or eggs. I went to my mom in anger and told her that I was hungry but there wasn't anything to eat.

She told my sister and me to go set the table, while she went into the room to pray. We followed her instructions and began to set the table. As we were placing the silverware on the table, I heard someone knock at the door. I ran to get my mom, shouting, "Mom, someone is at the door."

My mom asked who was at the door and opened it. One of them said, "I am here to bring you food."

All three of us started crying. They brought boxes and boxes of food inside. The excitement of being able to eat was so phenomenal, and from that day forward, I believed in prayer. We sat at the table and had dinner together as a family.

As a child I didn't realize how much of a blessing my mom was to me. She was a strong, intelligent, hard working, woman of God. She had to take care of us alone, work extremely hard, and paid bills that she never had enough money for. We had our lights, water, and gas cut off at one point or another, but my mom found a way to have them turned back on.

After the car accident, I didn't visit my dad anymore. He called to talk to me, and mailed me letters, but I hadn't seen him in a while. My mom asked me if I wanted to sue her for what my injuries incurred due to the accident. I said, "No," until she explained that when I turned eighteen years old, I would receive money with interest. I made a claim with my mom's insurance and we had to go back and forth to court.

During that time, my dad was released from prison on good behavior. Things were about to be altered in my life once again. I wondered if him coming home was good or bad. I questioned whether he might still be an abuser, an alcoholic, and an adulterer.

Everything seemed to be fine for the first few weeks, until he became angry and decided to abuse my mom. He created fear in me again. What he didn't realize is that I was a little older, so I thought differently than we did when I was younger. I ran to my neighbor's house for every altercation and called the police. I truly despised him and was disappointed that my mom wouldn't stand up for herself. Once again, life went on like nothing ever happened.

My mom went to work, and my sister was at a friend's house. I was at home alone with my dad. I was sitting on the floor watching television, in the living room. My dad came down from his room and proceeded to tickle me. My heart was rushing from the distress. He knew how I felt about him kissing me in my mouth and tickling me, I was never comfortable with that. He laid on top of me and asked me to breathe into his nostrils. I began to pray, asking God to please send my sister home.

My sister walked through the door, my dad immediately jumped up. He grabbed my sister and began to play with her. I went into my bedroom crying. I had to think fast, so I went to ask my dad if my sister and I could go to the corner store. He said, "Yes."

I called my sister into the room and asked her to pack her bag with as many clothes as she could fit. I told her that I would answer him if he asked us why we had backpacks, but he didn't ask.

As we walked to the store, I felt disgusted, flabbergasted, and nervous, because of what I had encountered. I didn't know if my plans were going to work, and I didn't want my sister to sense what I was going through, while I was going over my plans with her. As my sister went into the store, I went to the pay phone and called my aunt.

I immediately started to weep as I told her what had transpired. I asked her if she could come pick us up from the corner store. Once she arrived, she jumped out of the vehicle, ran over to us, and embraced us with a hug. As we walked back to the car, I expressed to her how I didn't want to go back home or leave my sister there alone. I was very fearful of the thought of leaving my sister at home alone. I had to protect my sister like I protected myself, since my oldest brother wasn't there anymore. He lived with his biological dad by this time.

My aunt called my mom to tell her what was going on, so that my mom wouldn't worry about us. My mom asked to speak with me. I was actually warming some oatmeal in the microwave, when I went to the phone. She told me that she was coming to pick me up.

I said, "I can't go back." Emotions of darkness captivated me as I began to tell her exactly what occurred while I was home alone with my dad.

She said, "I've already lost my son, I can't lose my girls, too." She told me that she loved me, that she was coming to my aunt's house after work, and that she was sorry that I had to experience that pain.

My mom came to my aunt's house after work, and when she walked through the door, she hugged my sister and me at the same time. She had finally decided to divorce my dad. Life didn't really change much because he was never around anyways. I was glad to see her stand up for herself. She always did better without him around.

I had to appear in court for the car accident lawsuit we had in process. I asked my attorney if I could see the judge in his chambers.

As my attorney walked me to the judge's chambers, no one knew what I wanted to ask him. He invited me to have a seat and asked what was on my mind.

I said, "I would like to buy a house with the money awarded to my sister and me."

He asked me, "Why are you thinking of that at such a young age."

I explained how tired I was of moving and changing schools, and how I wanted to see my mom happy for once.

He asked me, "How does your sister feel about it?"

I wasn't sure, so he requested for her to come into his chambers. She actually wanted the same thing, so the judge granted us our wish.

When I was fourteen we won the lawsuit and instantly started looking for homes. We found a beautiful home in Oak Park, Mich., with three bedrooms, two bathrooms, and a partially finished basement located on a street named Sussex. The day we moved into our home was another one of the happiest moments that I could remember as a teenager. We didn't have to live with anyone else; we lived in a suburb area; and we had stability.

Chapter Three

Bedazzled Vestments with Interwoven Stratums

In 1989 we moved into our new home. It was also my first year of high school, which I was excited to begin with a fresh start. I was the same broken adolescent with partially healed scars from my life situations. The underlying problems of anger, bitterness, rage, rejection, disappointment, and instability had yet to be addressed.

Although I was a nice person, I was hurting on the inside and trying to figure out how to balance my various emotions. What I encountered as a young girl affected me deeply and made me defensive and defiant during my adolescent years. I adopted a victim mentality from my childhood trauma, which enabled me to validate my behavior.

Just when I assumed that our lives were becoming healthier, my mom met a guy named Keith Simpson. When they started dating, I was skeptical about how their affiliation was going to affect my sister and me. I wanted to give him a chance to demonstrate his character before I judged him. He revealed his true character early on in their relationship. I assumed that my mom would have noticed similar characteristics in Keith that my dad displayed, but she did not.

In 1990, Keith and my mom had a wedding that my sister and I weren't a part of. My mom was in denial about his behavior toward my sister and me. He did things such as take my mom to dinner and not think of us. He would bring food for the two of them to our home, while my sister and I sat there with nothing to eat. They stayed in their bedroom together whenever they entered the home. It was like we were two teams against each other, when my sister and I were only asking to feel like we belonged in our own home.

Shortly after marriage, he became very physically, mentally, and verbally abusive. I couldn't understand why it was happening again, especially after going to the judge asking for a more peaceful life. Those years were the worst years for my mom and me. I didn't trust her decisions; I was extremely angry with her; and I didn't want to hear anything she had to tell me.

I decided to always hang out with friends so that I was only home for bed. My friends were going through different challenges, but we were all there for each other. The hardest part for me was going home at the end of the day. I didn't know what I was going to walk into. I couldn't get involved with what my mom was going through with Keith because it was overwhelming.

One day a group of friends decided to stay the night over at another friend's house for a girls' night out. We were all close to her dad because he was always around. Many of us didn't have a dad around for different reasons. He asked me if I wanted to go to the store with him. I agreed and told my sister that I was going.

On our way to the store, which was only several blocks away, he pulled over, put the car in park, and started talking to me. The music was playing very faintly. Seconds later, he climbed over and was on top of me in the passenger seat. He covered my mouth, asked me not to scream and raped me. I remember thinking not again, I thought he was different. I froze and was extremely shocked with tears running down my face. Numerous thoughts ran through my head. We never made it to the store.

Immediately after, he had a blank look on his face as if he was nervous about what was going to happen next. I should've jumped out of the car and ran home but I didn't. I asked him to take me home instead of returning back to his home. He asked me not to say anything to anyone. As soon as I walked through the door of my home, I went into the bathroom and washed my body for a long period of time. I went into my bedroom with thoughts of what happened, praying that my sister and the other girls were okay. I cried myself to sleep.

The next morning, when my sister came home from the sleep over, I asked her if we could get our other friends together. So, we were able to get all of the girls back together again. I told them what had transpired, and all of the girls, including my sister started sharing about what happened to them. We went to tell our parents, and later on that night we had a neighborhood meeting.

Instead of the meeting focusing on what happened to us girls, the parents discussed my behavior, which ignored the problem that we were confronting. I left feeling like a villain because the parents felt as if I was a bad influence on their children. We all were doing things such as sneaking out of the house, skipping classes, and going to house parties. I was dealing with a stepfather who didn't care for my sister or me, and I was raped the day before by someone I trusted. Yet, no one ever thought to ask me if I was okay.

I remember walking in on a conversation that one of the mother's was having a few days later. When I walked into the room I over heard her say that I was probably lying. The disappointment that I felt in that moment was horrific. I would never lie to anyone about something like that.

My mom took me to the police station to make a police report. I had to go to court, and the defendant pleaded guilty with my case. He was given a certain amount of time on probation. His daughter walked to school the same way we walked to school. She would scream out rude things to me while walking up the street. She didn't realize how much I wished I could've erased that day or how often I played it over in my head, thinking maybe I shouldn't have gone to the store with her dad or maybe I should've just stayed at home. I admired her family, only to find out her dad was a pervert.

Several months later, the defendant's daughter and her friends jumped my sister on the way home from school. I was so upset, so I planned for my sister to fight her back on the way home from school on the following day. I met my sister and one of our friends at Coney Island, so that I could tell them the plan. As they continued to walk home like they normally would, I walked in the alley. I found a forty-ounce beer bottle and broke it. As my sister met up with the girls who jumped her, I was approaching the end of the alley. I ran toward them with the broken bottle and said they'd have to deal with me if they tried to jump my sister again. My sister and the defendant's daughter fought one on one, until the police came. We all ran home so that we wouldn't get in any trouble.

That day, I thought about how close I had come to going to jail. I decided that I had to learn to be in control and not let circumstances overtake me. I had to figure out how to balance my emotions, my thoughts, and my behaviors. I was tired of going around a never-ending roller coaster. So, I went to school, worked at home after school, did hair for my classmates, and made a decent amount of money for a high schooler. The last straw was when my mom moved out with her abusive husband, leaving my fifteen-year-old sister home with me.

I dropped out of school, picked up another job, and worked at a nursing home styling senior citizens hair. My classmates continued to come to my home to get their hair styled. I decided to go to cosmetology school, which accepted high school dropouts. The bills were so overwhelming that I needed to work more hours, so I stayed in cosmetology school for a short period of time. We were barely eating or paying the bills. I was upset about where I was in life.

A year later, in 1993, I turned eighteen years old. I received a check for seventy-five dollars from the lawsuit. I called my mom and asked her why my check was so small. She said, "I used it to pay the mortgage because I didn't have it." The judge explained that if I bought the house, my mom had to pay the mortgage. Which means that a deposit was put down on the house from the money I was awarded, and she made monthly installments until I turned eighteen years old. I wanted them to pay for it in full, but I was a minor and the judge disagreed. My mom relied on the payments from my lawsuit instead of paying the installments agreed upon.

My plans went out of the window, I was very disappointed. I assumed that I would be able to catch up on my bills with the money received. I asked her if she could refinance the house under her name because I was having some financial difficulties. She said, "Yes."

We refinanced the house and agreed that my sister and I would get the house back in our names once we figured out our finances. That home was supposed to be our family home, so if any of us ever needed a place to live, we had a place regardless. Shortly after the agreement, she and Keith moved back into the home. Things didn't improve, they got worse. He threw me out of the house on several occasions because my mom's name was on the house. I couldn't understand how my mom allowed things like that to happen.

The time came for my sister and me to ask for the home back. We went to my mom to ask her to switch the names back over. She said, "No." I felt betrayed and cried many nights. I tried to express myself to her, but she wouldn't take responsibility for her actions. She always shut down any conversation about the house or the things that happened to us when we younger, including her leaving my sister with me at such a young age, and then sealed it with a prayer.

Some years later, Keith and my mom sold our home. We actually didn't even know that they sold the home until after it was sold. They took a large sum of money from the profits received and used it for a deposit on a rental property for themselves. I didn't receive any money from my mom when she sold our home.

The foundation of trust was broken with both of my parents at that point. I really didn't understand how a mom and dad could be so dysfunctional in raising children, until I had children of my own. Experiencing heartaches with no time to breathe or heal was very detrimental for me. It was during those times of disappointments, heartaches, and pain that I found myself more eager to make a difference in my life.

As a teenager going into adulthood, I truly wanted to find out what giving my life to the Lord was all about. I went to church regularly, served in the ministry, and was very familiar with the people there, but I wanted a more personal relationship with God. I dropped down on my knees and began to pray. I asked God to come into my heart and show me how to be the young lady he created me to be. I told him that I didn't know how or where to start, but I gave him my complete self. From that day forward, I began to see a change in my character. I desired to treat people with the love that God allowed me to experience in that moment.

Still, I didn't realize that although I had accepted God into my heart, I was a hot mess from the things that had transpired in my childhood. God anticipated healing me, but guilt crippled me, shame hid me, and pride reigned. I was the same person on the outside, with changes taking place inside. I couldn't see myself the way God saw me. I didn't feel worthy of his love, but he loved me anyway.

Chapter Four

Celebratory Array with Ruffled Fibers

In 1993, I got engaged to Timothy Hicks, who I had met a few years previously through his aunt. When she introduced us, I didn't think he was my type. Once I got to know him, he seemed very sweet, bashful, and quiet. We started hanging out together on a daily basis. We had sex early on, so I believe that my emotions were wrapped around an orgasm rather than love. I didn't understand the difference when I was younger, so I automatically assumed that it was love. After going through ups and downs in our relationship, I thought that it was love, but really, it was getting what I wanted for the moment.

We were at a hotel when he got down on his knee to ask me to marry him. At the time, we were young and ignorant about relationships and didn't even know who we were as individuals. I had put my security in Timothy to make me happy as I carried insecurities within myself. I accepted behaviors in our relationship to feel accepted. I also controlled situations to keep from getting hurt.

We both were two broken people from two different ends of the spectrum. We had experienced abandonment, insecurities, and dysfunction and came together with no direction. We carried baggage from our childhood, and we didn't deal with ourselves before we decided to knit our hearts together.

His mother gave birth to him and his twin on her fourteenth birthday. His biological dad left the scene after he was born. I never met his dad during the fifteen years that we were married, nor did he ever talk about him. Timothy's mom married his stepdad when he was two years old. He was a great example of a family man, and always made fair judgments when it came to me. Unfortunately, they were also divorced after many years of marriage.

My mom was abused on many occasions. My dad was in and out of jail, our home, and my life during my upbringing. When he was around, he brought chaos. We seemed to have more peace, happiness, and calm in our home when my dad was gone. My mom seemed to get on her feet when my dad was away, and as soon as he returned life was hectic. Even though we struggled financially when my dad was gone, we suffered mentally, emotionally, and physically when he was around.

On September 28, 1994, in the early morning, we drove my dad's car to Toledo, Ohio, to elope. Both of my parents knew that we were going to get married. Timothy asked me to keep our marriage a secret, because his mother didn't want him to marry me, and I agreed. Just before I signed our marriage license, I remembered a conversation that my mom and I had just days before. She told me that I should reconsider my decision to marry him because he was going to cheat on me. She said he seemed sneaky. I told her that he was nothing like the men she had been involved with, and I ignored her advice as I proceeded to sign the certificate.

After signing the necessary documents, I was married moments later. On our way back to the city of Detroit, he told me that we couldn't move in together until a little later because we were keeping our marriage a secret. So many thoughts were going through my mind. Did I make the right decision? That day didn't feel like the best day in my life. Should I have listened to my mom?

I really didn't have a good example of a father or father figure in my life. I was young and thought I knew everything. I actually thought that I was smarter than my mom because she put up with things I said that I would never accept in my life. Yet, I accepted Timothy's request for me to remain silent about our marriage. That was stupid of me.

While living apart, we managed to go to church together regularly. We served in the church and hung out with the young married couples. We went bowling, to the movies, to dinner, and traveled. I served in the nursery. He was an usher and later became the head of the deacon's board. We had so much fun as a church family and made the best out of our relationship. We went over to the pastor's house just about every Sunday for dinner. We played games, told jokes, and ate good food.

A year later Timothy and I separated, we just weren't seeing eye to eye. As a married couple, we made false threats of divorce. We didn't have relationship goals, so we both crossed the line of respect too many times. Things appeared so beautiful around others but were so rocky behind the scenes. He wanted to live like a bachelor with a wife. He wasn't providing for me, he hung out with his friends regularly, and he came around when he wanted to have sex. Why shouldn't he? It was free, flexible, and convenient. I was tired of being a part-time wife, so I told him that I couldn't do it anymore.

Shortly after our separation, I found out that I was pregnant. I had so many emotions that came over me at once. I was happy because I had another life growing inside of me. I was sad because I didn't want to raise my children the way I was raised. I was nervous because I wasn't going to have an abortion, and I didn't want my children to have different fathers.

Not long after finding out that I was pregnant, my friend Mona Sherell, told me that she saw Timothy with another young lady at the mall. Mona saw him hiding from her, so she called me immediately. When I tried to contact him, he wouldn't answer my phone calls. I was so hurt and disappointed with multiple thoughts running through my mind. We had only been separated for a few weeks, plus I thought things would change when I told him that I was expecting his baby. By this time his whole family knew that we were married.

He had just been at my house, filling out job applications. I thought about looking for the application to see if I could find anything suspicious. When I looked, I noticed that one of his references was an unfamiliar name Natalie Betters. I called her number multiple times, but I didn't get an answer. I was panicking about how I didn't want to have a baby without a father.

The next morning, I called Natalie again, and she answered. I asked her how she knew my husband, and she told me that he was her man and was right there next to her sleeping. I asked her if she knew that he was married. She said "No." She told me that she had been at his house on multiple occasions, and no one ever mentioned that he was married.

I was extremely annoyed and disappointed with him and his lack of concern for me. I went into the kitchen and took a knife out of the drawer and set it on the ledge in my foyer. I was contemplating stabbing him when he walked through the door. He called me several hours later. I asked him to bring me something to eat. He told me that he couldn't bring me anything until later. I had time to rationalize my emotions as I considered our innocent baby and the rest of my future. It didn't make sense for me to ponder hurting him for making his own decisions. I needed to value myself and walk away.

I severed all communication with him, until I was approximately twenty weeks pregnant. I was almost five months along, when I reached out to his mom about the ultrasound. I didn't want to withhold information from him about our baby girl. So, I mailed a picture of the ultrasound to his mom's house. Once they received it, he kept stopping by my home, calling, and leaving messages. I watched him come to my door, knock, wait, and leave.

I experienced extreme financial challenges during my pregnancy. My lights were disconnected, my water was cut off, and I had to keep my food inside of a cooler so that I could eat. I was so thankful for one of my friends from church who was there with me. She stayed multiple nights at a time to keep me company. She brought candles to get me through the night, and I made it through those tough times. I made the best out of what I had every day. It was amazing for me to have someone alongside me during this challenging time. She wasn't obligated to be there during this time in my life. She and I prayed together believing God for a change.

As the months went on, Timothy kept pursuing me. One day, an unknown number popped up on my phone. I answered, and he pleaded with me to please just hear him out. I was six months pregnant and trying to survive this experience alone, so I listened briefly. We came up with a plan to meet at the mall once a week so that Timothy could give me money to help prepare for the arrival of our little girl. The more he met me, the more he kept speaking of being a better husband and a great dad.

On December 16, 1995, I had my baby shower at my aunt's house. I was almost eight months pregnant with a due date of February 9, 1996. Timothy and I decided to reconcile our marriage since I was going to deliver our baby soon. He had been more attentive to me and had made various promises about how he was going to be a great husband and father. I wanted to give him a chance to make a difference in our relationship. I wondered if he could've been a great husband and an awesome dad that he said he could be.

During that time, I received a call from Natalie, the young lady who was on his list of references. She told me that she was pregnant, and that Timothy wanted her to get an abortion. I listened at first, then asked if having an abortion is what she wanted. She said "No." I prayed with her. We prayed for God to heal her heart, give her direction, and for her to have a healthy pregnancy. My heart was hurting to hear that Timothy had gotten her pregnant. I didn't want his past mistakes to destroy our family, when we had recently reconciled. I felt like the baby the two of them had conceived didn't ask to be here, and that the decision of an abortion needed to be made by both parties. Timothy should not have pressured her to do it just to cover up his dirt.

Celebratory Array With Ruffled Fibers

I actually had a flashback of some incidents that happened during my pregnancy that began to make sense. I went to the mall to shop for maternity clothes as I grew larger. When I walked into the store, a young lady approached me with such a beautiful smile and asked me if she could assist me in any way. As I was trying on garments, she told me if they looked cute or not. I remember so vividly asking her to zip up my pink romper. While we were talking and laughing, she began to tell me about her boyfriend. Her boyfriend worked in the mall; my husband worked in the mall. Her boyfriend worked at Little Caesars; my husband worked at Little Caesars. I didn't put two and two together until the day she told me that she was pregnant, it was Natalie.

Another time, I was at the pay phone in the mall talking to Timothy. I looked up and a young lady was staring at me. Jokingly, I said, "You must be dating this young lady standing across from me, because she keeps staring at me." I didn't recognize that she was the same young lady who assisted me in the store as I tried on my garments, it was Natalie.

During my last weeks of pregnancy, I started seeing Natalie when I went to my doctors' appointments, restaurants, and other places around town. When I mentioned it to Timothy, he told me that it was over between the two of them, and he didn't want to have anything to do with her. I told him that even though we had mended our relationship, he needed to be there for his baby. He told me that it may not be his baby. So, I suggested for him to get a DNA test, if he didn't believe it was his baby.

On February 14, 1996, I was in Providence Hospital in Southfield, Mich., in labor. Timothy, my mom, and my siblings were in the room with me, while other family members and friends were in the waiting area. I was in an enormous amount of pain for approximately nine hours. I delivered our baby girl, who had big beautiful brown eyes and a full head of hair, at 12:05 a.m. February 15, 1996, only five minutes after Valentine's Day. At birth, my daughter didn't cry, but made a noise as if to say, "I'm here." A love came over me that I'd never felt before as I embraced her presence. It was one of the most precious moments in my life. I felt so much joy and happiness as huge tears pounded down my cheeks.

On February 17, 1996, two days after my beautiful baby girl entered the world, it was time to go home from the hospital. It was Timothy's birthday, so we celebrated with cake, ice cream, and the new edition to our family. Timothy actually shares his birthday with his identical twin brother and his mom. I believed that Timothy and I had another opportunity to start fresh and maybe I hadn't made a mistake after all.

Timothy seemed to be very attentive to our new edition and to me. I didn't forget Timothy's abandonment and that he had gotten another woman pregnant, but I also didn't want that to be my focus. Instead, I embraced the picture that I had painted in my own head, which was that we could move on and live happily ever after. Looking back over my life during that time, I realize that I lived in my marriage based off of what I wanted, rather than accepting the reality of what was going on right in front of my face.

A few weeks later, I received a call from someone at the hospital stating that Timothy was in a car accident. I rushed to the hospital, and he was stable. He began to tell me what happened in the accident. Strangely, many young women kept appearing at the hospital, and I overheard them talking about the accident. I was so concentrated on his being coherent, that I didn't indulge in the miscellaneous communication. Timothy was sent home that same day with instructions to rest.

Several months later, a call came in that Natalie was in labor with Timothy's baby. We were lying down when he looked into my eyes and held me close to him as he said, "I don't have to go."

I said, "Yes you do. She needs you. Go."

He got up and went to the hospital. My heart was overwhelmed with excruciating pain and enough tears streamed down my face to make a pond. The insecurity of not being good enough attacked my emotions.

Timothy called shortly after Natalie gave birth to a little girl. Immediately, I felt jealous, angry, emotional, insecure, and offended. I was still going through postpartum depression myself and my emotions were all over the place. The agonizing pain that I felt in my heart was intolerable. I cried and prayed to God, asking him to please give me the strength to handle that situation.

As Timothy walked through the door that evening, I immediately asked if we could talk. He agreed, and I shared my heart. I asked him to give me some time to heal before he brought his daughter around because I wanted to treat her like she was my own daughter. I also told him that I would never keep him from going to see her.

He said, "I understand."

It took me approximately three months to embrace her like she was my own.

Just before I was able to bury my pride, my thoughts entrapped me, and the feeling of embarrassment crippled me. I decided to embrace the fact that I was pregnant again with my second baby. This pregnancy wasn't planned and my daughter was only three months old. I went to my doctor's appointment for my routine visit, and the doctor told me that I was pregnant. I was so shocked!

I felt like I needed to be an example of love to my children. So, I started getting our girls together to play with each other, spend weekends together, and grow up together. The more Timothy's baby came around, the more I felt like she was my own baby girl.

It came time for me to give birth again. On February 19, 1997, a handsome baby boy was born, who weighed 5 lbs. 4 oz. He had slanted, dark brown eyes, extremely long eyelashes, and a head full of dark beautiful hair.

I was immediately attacked by postpartum depression, again. I had never experienced depression like that before. I was happy and sad at the same time. I couldn't control my emotions, and I wanted to sleep continuously. I truly thank God for my mom and my sister. My sister was pregnant herself. They both pitched in where they needed too and helped me as much as they could. They changed his diapers, and my oldest daughter was already potty-trained. They made sure that my son had his bottles and that my daughter ate in a timely matter. My sister took them with her often. I started coming out of that depression about a month later.

It was time for my sister to have her baby. On March 21, 1997, I was in the delivery room when she gave birth to a beautiful baby girl, who weighed 5 lbs. 1oz. and measured 19 inches long. She was very tiny with big beautiful eyes and a precious smile. I wanted to protect her like she was my own daughter.

A year later, I remember going to dinner with Timothy. I went into the restroom because I couldn't stand up straight. I was cramping extremely badly. I remember thinking, "It feels like I'm going to have a miscarriage, and I'm not pregnant." I called my doctor the following day and made an appointment. Sure enough, I was three months pregnant.

Timothy and I were avoiding dealing with severe underlying issues in our relationship because I was pregnant again, again, and again. It was time to deliver our third baby on February 13, 1999. I gave birth to a handsome baby boy, who was fair-skinned with red hair and slanted eyes. On September 23, 2000, I delivered our fourth child, a beautiful baby girl, who had very big brown eyes and curly hair. On October 29, 2002, our fifth baby was born, a beautiful baby girl with slanted eyes, dark straight hair, weighing in at 8 lbs. 4oz. and measuring 22 inches long.

Within seven years I gave birth to five children. During those years of either being pregnant or delivering a baby, I thought that I was doing what a woman was supposed to do. I was married, I worked, I cooked when I had the energy, and I cleaned when I wasn't feeling depressed. I was broken, trying to heal myself with the sensational feeling of love that I gained after each child.

All along I was married to someone who lived a double life. I convinced myself to believe a lie when I knew the truth from the start. I brought five children into a lifestyle that was extremely similar to my own childhood, a childhood that I never desired to duplicate. How could I explain this to my children? I believed that there was hope, even when he showed me consistently that he didn't love me. He couldn't love me because he didn't love himself. I blamed myself for so long for what went wrong. But I don't blame myself anymore, and I don't blame him either. I look at it as something I went through to get where I am today.

Chapter Five

Elaborate Masquerades with Closures

By the age of twenty-eight, I had five children, my marriage was malfunctioning, and I was under the impression that I needed to be a perfect Christian. I started noticing traits of my childhood duplicating themselves in my lifestyle. We struggled to keep food in our home, and we moved around the city on countless occasions. Regardless of how much we worked, we never had enough. I was tremendously oblivious to what was going on right in front of my face.

I received a call from my doctor, who asked to see me in his office. When I arrived the following day, he asked me to have a seat. My heart was beating fast, and I felt anxiety sneaking up on me. He said, "Your husband is cheating on you." My heart dropped! He explained the importance of my protecting myself. When I walked back into the lobby, where Timothy was sitting, I couldn't look at him. As we walked to the car in silence as so many incidents came back to mind.

There were many signs of Timothy blatantly cheating on me that I overlooked on numerous instances. He worked many hours of overtime; he mostly slept when he returned home; he was extremely secluded. The people around us had no idea of what was going on inside of our home. We went to church regularly, and I wore a smile on my face. I had regret in my heart and a defense mechanism with my actions in various altercations.

I often ask myself now, why I didn't just leave him when I found out that another woman was pregnant? Was I that insecure? Was my motive to prove others wrong? Were the feelings of rejection from my childhood extending over into my adulthood and my marriage? Did I stay to prove that I had it all together or to save myself embarrassment of what others would think of me? I totally believe it was all the above.

After having that conversation with my doctor, I still didn't leave. Where was I going to go? Who could I talk to? I had too many children to leave him. These were the things that I told myself. As time went on, things got worse. He invited his women to church and my children's birthday parties. He became more and more disrespectful. I felt numb. I was breathing but chose to deny my emotions to remain strong. I was literally only existing, and I allowed time to slip away right in my presence. I totally believed that things were going to get better.

Two years later, I was resting and Timothy's phone rang. His cousin's name popped up on the screen, so I answered. It wasn't his cousin. The woman on the other end of the phone asked, "Who is this?" I said, "This is his wife with five children. Who are you?" She told me that she was his woman, and she asked when he got married, because they had been dating for six months. Timothy was laying on the sofa, so I took him the phone. As soon as she said, "Hello," he hung up, sat up, and asked me what she had said.

I remember that heartbreaking day as if it was yesterday. I was in school and working at a boutique at the time. Once I gave him his phone back, I ran upstairs with tears aggressively streaming down my face. I had an excruciating pain in my heart that felt like someone was stabbing me repeatedly in the exact same place. I couldn't take it anymore. I explained to my boss the next day that I wouldn't be of any help to her that day and that I needed to figure my life out. She said that she had an apartment available that was attached to her home. I asked her when could I move in, and she said, "Today."

I didn't know what to say to my children. I didn't want to be the mother who spoke negatively to my children about their dad. I told them that their dad would always love them but that our relationship wasn't working, so we had to move into an apartment. We moved that day into our two-bedroom, mother-in-law quarters. Our lives changed in a matter of minutes, and immediately, I snapped into survival mode.

I decided to get creative with doing things to keep my children active. I wanted to make sure that my children knew how important they were, so we walked to a nearby parking structure and wrote music. So many heartfelt songs were made during that season of our lives. They actually had someone make a music CD for them, but we never did anything with it.

We continued to attend church at a different location, and one day, I received a call from the pastor's wife from the previous church. She told me that a young lady came to the church and asked for my number. She wanted permission to give it to her before she gave out my number. I told her that it was fine to give my number to her. The lady called me and began to apologize for being with Timothy for the past two years. She assumed I left him because I found out about her. I told her I left because of multiple reasons, and she wasn't one of them. She was married and angry when she found out it was a different phone call that motivated me to leave. I asked her if I could pray with her. We prayed! As soon as we hung up the phone, my phone rang again. It was her husband asking me if we could pay his wife and Timothy back by having a relationship. I immediately hung up on him! I couldn't believe what I had just heard.

Although I was trying to act as if nothing ever happened, I felt it at night. I would toss and turn and couldn't sleep. I was scared of failing my children. I felt guilty for taking them from their dad and terrified of what the future held. I kept striving. I was in fashion design school full-time, and I continued to work at the boutique, until I decided that I wanted my own design studio.

A year later, I moved into a house, opened a design studio, and had our clothes selling in two stores at the mall. Life seemed to be going okay, until I decided to help Timothy out. He called me saying that he wanted to come home to be with his children, and if things didn't work out he would leave. I thought about it over and over again, and finally I agreed! "Everyone makes mistakes," I rationalized thinking that maybe he had learned his lesson once again. The kids were so happy, and that's what mattered the most to me at that time.

It was the worst year we had together. He didn't keep his word, and we argued every day. It was more dysfunctional for my children with him there. I started meeting with my children daily. We read the Bible, prayed, and talked about our highs and lows for the day. I started having dreams of Timothy about things that were happening the following day. I knew that I had to get out of that marriage, but how? I procrastinated and stayed longer.

The plant where he was employed at was closing. He could have chosen to have the company relocate him or take a buyout with a severance pay. He decided to take a buy-out and find his own job. He asked me what he could give me since he was going to have a lump sum of money. I told him that I wanted to do a seven-piece collection. Which is a clothing collection that consists of seven pieces that I designed and wanted to get in stores for retail for the following season.

Our family drove to New York to put in my sample order for my collection on January 29, 2008. We stayed for seven days to take the kids site seeing. We went to the largest Toys R Us. We visited the most popular fabric stores in the garment district. We made the best of our trip not realizing that it would be our last family trip.

Timothy and I didn't have any fire left between the two of us. We both knew that it was time to move on. Although, we kept pushing family togetherness for the appearance and for our children. After returning home, the next few months were very difficult. Timothy stayed out later than he normally would've, and he was intoxicated. Our children had questions about why their dad was laying on the bathroom floor asleep, when they were getting ready for school. I finally realized that me staying wasn't helping my children at all, rather it was hurting them tremendously.

It was time for me to go back to New York to pick up my collection. We had already scheduled a time to return before we left. Unfortunately, when it came time to go back, Timothy wouldn't take me. So, I asked him if he could help me with the money to go, since we had already placed an order. I didn't want to lose the money previously invested. He told me that he could give me one hundred dollars, but I owed over seven hundred dollars for the collection. I told my sister that I was going but I only had one hundred dollars. She had twenty-five dollars. She was going through some changes in her own life and wanted to get away as well. I left my children, and she brought hers.

We left Michigan in the middle of the night with one hundred and twenty-five dollars total. I still can't explain how I overcame the fear to do what we did. We drove eleven hours, we had to stop to get gas four times. We ate with every stop.

By the time we made it to New York, we had twenty dollars left. My niece and nephew were hungry, so I told my sister to take them in to Subway to eat. I walked around to the other side of the shopping center, talking to God. I was rambling back and forth with so many thoughts of what to do next. I called my sister-in-law and we prayed together. We left there and drove to the nearest hotel.

We went inside of the hotel to ask if we could use the restroom. They said, "Not unless you're a guest." We went back to the minivan. It was late, and we were extremely tired. I told my sister, niece, and nephew to go to sleep, while I watched our surroundings. I fell asleep at some point and remember waking up trying to figure out what to do next.

We called a friend and told her what was going on. She wired us one hundred dollars. We went into Walmart to wash up and change clothes. During that time, I received a phone call from a long-time friend who lived in New York. She invited us over for dinner. Once we arrived, she told me that her aunt knew that we were coming. When I spoke with her aunt she told me that God told her that I was coming and that she needed to make sure that I was taken care of while I was there. She gave us food and a place to sleep. We had so much fun hanging out.

A few days later, it was time for me to go pick up my clothing collection, and I didn't have the money to pay for it. I received a call from another friend who told me that she had vision about my being a billionaire. She and her husband wanted to sow a seed of a few hundred dollars into my life and wired it to me. When the cashier asked me what the amount was, I said, "Two hundred dollars." When he started counting the money out to me, he kept counting past two hundred until he reached nine hundred dollars. They sent enough money to pay for my collection and to make it back home. I was so amazed!

As we were on the road to return home, I made up my mind that I wasn't going to settle for less in my marriage any longer. I called a friend in Las Vegas and asked her if we could stay with her for thirty days to give me time to get on my feet. She said, "Yes." It was time for me to turn my life around, but how could I do that with five children, no money, or a concrete plan?

Once I returned home, Timothy denied my request to take the children to Las Vegas. Two days later he came to me and said, "I've been thinking about what you asked. Yes, you can take them." I had a birthday coming up, so I decided to plan a going away birthday party.

The night before my birthday, my children stayed the night over some family members home to give me a relaxed evening without the kids. Timothy didn't come home until the morning of my birthday. When he arrived the morning of my birthday, he asked me to have sex. I denied him because I couldn't handle the feelings that came along with sex. I told him that our relationship was over. I would no longer be his doormat.

Chapter Six

Intricate Gear Ready for Tussle

After a heartfelt going away birthday celebration in July 2008, I packed up my minivan with four of my five children, my sister, and her two children. We drove to North Carolina to pick my oldest daughter, who had spent the summer there with her godparents. We continued on to South Carolina to visit my aunt and uncle for a few days before we traveled to Las Vegas. I sent out a text message to my family and friends saying, "I am on my way to my destiny. Can anyone help us get there?" I told them that I was on my way to my destiny, because I believed that life was going to change for my children and me. I didn't want to stay in Michigan because I didn't feel like I had a great support system. I'd rather go somewhere unfamiliar and trust God with my decisions, than to be with family and feel like no one was there. The support system was different from when my children were babies.

Our drive was fun, we played games, and drove through many states in three days. We were able to make our trip a great experience. Every time we stopped to get gas, we were able to get food. We were low on funds but always had just enough.

I hadn't processed the fact that I was about to become a single parent until we arrived in Las Vegas. I realized that we couldn't stay where we had planned to live because there were too many of us. My sister came just to help me drive, so once she and her children left, it was my babies and me with no place to go, no money left, and two outfits each, including the clothes we were wearing.

I called my mom, and she suggested that my uncle could probably help me. I called him after hanging up the phone with her and found out I had an aunt in Las Vegas. I contacted her and told her that my children and I were in the city. She asked me to meet her at church the following day, so we did. She introduced us to a deacon at her church, who wanted to show us one of his rental properties after church. As we walked through the home, he said, "We normally rent this house out for thirteen hundred dollars per month."

I immediately responded, "I can't afford anything close to that."

He said, "Not for you; that's the normal going rate. We are going to give you this house for free until you can get on your feet."

This house had five bedrooms, and my children and I lived there for seven months. During that time, I joined a church, a women's book club, and searched for work on a daily basis. I was determined not live on welfare, so we only received food stamps. After being in Las Vegas for about three months, I remember facing the challenge of not having enough to pay my light bill. I called the church to ask for prayer, I was told that I had to make an appointment.

I asked, "For prayer?"

The lady said, "I'm sorry I thought you wanted your light bill paid." In order for the church to assist with any utilities it must first go through the pastor. She misunderstood my request, she prayed.

Later that night I met the women from my book club, and I began to tell them what happened earlier that day. Before I finished telling them how I really wanted to trust God in my situation, two ladies offered to help me. Both women came over to me and asked me how much my light bill cost. I told them the past due amount. They asked me to call the light company immediately. They wanted to pay my bill because they felt as if God put on their hearts to pay the total bill. I couldn't stop crying because I knew that my lights would've been turned off the following morning had they not helped me. I was determined to trust God. He continued to bless me through people.

Those ladies were such a blessing to my children and me. They saw the intentions of my heart. I wasn't trying to take advantage of anyone; I was trying to find a solution. We prayed, did Bible studies, played games, and ate together, weekly. I needed them during that season of my life.

My children wore the same two outfits to school every other day for seven months. Daily, I washed their clothes by hand and hung them on the line in the backyard to dry. I cooked breakfast and dinner often. We were very close and did everything together. The area that we lived in wasn't the best part of Las Vegas. We heard gun shots, regularly.

I can remember lying in bed crying for hours, feeling stupid for staying with their dad for as long as I did. I asked myself the question, "How could I have five children for anyone?" Now, raising them alone was extremely overwhelming. I love all of my children dearly, but the stress of being a single mom can be overwhelming. Children really don't realize the many sacrifices parents make so that they can have a normal childhood.

It was hard to find work, and I was living in someone's home and couldn't pay for it. I felt helpless, but I kept praying, no matter what I felt like. The peace that surpasses all understanding came alive in my bones. No longer a victim, I became a strong woman who was ready for what the world had to offer. I watched our lives go through a transition as I faced every situation on my knees in prayer before handling them in public.

My children didn't go to school near our home. I had to drive them thirty minutes each way, every day. They had school choice because the ratings of the schools around us were very poor. I remember trying to get my children involved immediately. All of my children were athletes in some way.

We met a man whose daughter had played for one of the best basketball programs in Las Vegas. It was the same team my daughter was trying out for with her middle school. She tried out and made the team. The coaches, teachers, and parents reached out to us to make sure that we had sponsorships for basketball. They also signed us up for the backpack lunches, which is when the school fills the child's backpack up with food at the end of the day on weekends. The sports team adopted us for Christmas and my children received so many gifts. It was unbelievable how a community came together on our behalf.

A couple from the church we were attending, also adopted us. They bought my babies clothes and gave me money to use for anything we needed. I was amazed at how our life continued to get better.

I continued to search for work. My uncle called me and said, "Kima, the Census Bureau is hiring. You need to come over to the recreational center immediately and put in an application." I rushed over, and I was hired to work for the government almost immediately. I worked for three months and found a condo for rent closer to my children's school. We moved in, and we were so excited. Life started to feel normal again, until three months later when I was laid off. I couldn't pay my rent. I was overwhelmed once again.

I packed up the kids and drove back to Detroit. I made another irrational decision because I didn't know what to do. Going back to Detroit was such a horrific experience. We bounced around between the homes of family and friends for three weeks. I was so unstable. The feeling of people being tired of us was so overbearing. My oldest daughter flew back for basketball. The rest of us drove back. As soon as we parked and went into the house, we heard someone knocking on the door. I opened the door, and it was an officer coming to evict us. I had driven for three days, and we are about to become homeless again. I didn't know what to do besides pray and ask for direction. I was extremely embarrassed and didn't know how to explain it to my children.

I sat them down and told them that we had to stick together. I went to sign up at the shelter, but I couldn't do it. I grabbed my children and apologized to them for this traumatic experience. We drove around trying to find a safe place to park so we could sleep. One of my close friends called me and told us to come to her home for a couple nights. During those days, I went out every day to find a way to help myself.

The State had a program for low income families that offered thirty days stay in a hotel, free of charge. They paid for my children and me to stay at a hotel with a kitchenette for a month. My social worker made it clear that once we reached the thirty days there was nothing else that they could do to assist me. I Believed in my heart that God was going to bless me with exactly what I needed.

Two weeks later, I received a called from a mom of one of my daughter's teammates. She asked me if I could share my story with her, so I did. She then asked me to meet her at a home that she owned. She was looking for tenants to occupy the home. I gathered the children together, and we drove to her home. We walked through the empty beautiful home. I loved it, as we were walking out, she dangled the keys in the air standing by the front door.

"I told her that I didn't work, but she told me that she believed in me, and all I needed to do was to keep striving, and good things would continue to come to me."

She gave me a lease to sign and told me I could break my rent into two payments every month. Just before moving into her home, I put an application in Walmart and did not get the job. The same week I moved into her home I found a job at Walmart, in a different location through a different teammates' parent. The following week I found a second job as a teacher's assistant. I went from having no job to having two jobs within two weeks. I worked midnights. I got off work in the morning went home to get showered and dressed for my other job. I never really had time to spend with my children aside from our daily meetings whenever our day permitted it, rather it was early in the morning, late in the evening, or my off days. I found time to hear about how their day. I met with my children's teachers to make sure they knew how important my children were to me. I couldn't meet the teachers individually, I had group conferences for each child.

All of my children were in one sport or another. I remember when my boys wanted to play football, and my friend knew someone who wanted to sponsor them. I never met the sponsor for them to be sponsored, I had to arrive early to stand in line. We went early in the morning before anyone else was there. Once the young lady who told me about the sponsorship showed up, she told me that the sponsors backed out. I decided to remain in line and allow the people who were registering the children to tell me no. It was our turn to approach the counter. I asked the lady if there was anything that I could do to have my boys registered, since we had waited in line so long. Just as I was about to turn and walk away with my boys, a man with a deep voice offered to pay for them. The gratitude I felt was overwhelming. I was extremely shocked, but thankful.

Life began to change for my family again. I was determined not to allow my childhood experiences to continue to influence my lifestyle, but I had to make better decisions to get different results.

I worked two jobs, went to my children's games, and tried to make sure I spent every dime of my money wisely. It came to a point where I needed to make more money. I needed a career. I felt like I was spinning my wheels, so I decided to go back to school for cosmetology.

I sat my children down again, and I told them that it was "do or die." We were drowning in bills, even though I was working so much. I told them that I needed to make a change in my life so we could make a difference in the world. The very next day I went to sign up for school. I knew I had to take school seriously so I could change our lives. In orientation, they told us that we could never be late, absent, or allow our grade point average to drop below a certain average.

I carefully thought about the rules and sat my babies down again to express the importance of my following the school's rules. I told them that I may not be able to attend as many games, but I would definitely attend as many as I could. At the time, I was still working two jobs. I turned in my resignation for my day job as a teacher's assistant, so I could focus on school. I told myself it was my time to shine. I needed to give my best efforts.

That year was extremely stressful. No one at school knew much about me because I didn't talk much. I had too much going on in my life, and school wasn't the place to share it. I dressed as if I were going to work every day. I did that to encourage myself. There were days when I would go to school with no food and no electricity at home and a broken down car. I had to wake up at three in the morning and get to the bus stop by 4:30 a.m. to make it to school by eight, but I was determined.

I remember my classmates talking about their lives. I couldn't join their conversations because I didn't want to get sidetracked from the actual reason I was there. After going to cosmetology school for so many hours, I had to start practicing on actual clients. It came time for me to go on the floor to take appointments because I had four hundred hours. So, when people called in for an appointment I serviced them as if I was in the salon.

I was on the floor three days a week. I was booked from the morning until it was time for me to leave. Some of my classmates wasn't as busy and treated me horribly, by lying on me, or provoking an innocent situation for me to respond. The only thing that kept me from responding to their behaviors was the fact that I had a plan. I had to remember that regardless of what happened, I was in control of my own successes and failures.

I was doing a client's hair, I shared with her how much I really wanted to go to the ABS show in Chicago, which is a large known beauty show for cosmetologist and students. By going to the show, I could purchase my tools, and get hands on education. She asked me if she could send me. I was amazed and said, "Yes." She actually booked my ticket at that very moment. By that time, I only had a few months left of school.

When I arrived in Chicago, my sister, god sister, and close friend came to see me. We met at the hotel and immediately went to dinner. While catching up, I remember getting on a subject about me. That conversation didn't go as well as anticipated, but I didn't think too much of it.

The next day I got ready in the bathroom. My friend wiped my face. I moved her hand and said, "Please don't invade my space."

I didn't consider my response earlier because I was at a point of my life where I started realizing that there's a certain amount of space that belongs only to me. It was up to me to allow her to touch my face or not.

It was time for us to go to the red-carpet event with Vidal Sassoon. As I got dressed, I chose to wear a necklace tied as a choker around my neck. My friend expressed how it wasn't the ideal look. I appreciated her opinion, but I still chose to wear the choker. Once again, I was just figuring out my self-worth. We had a phenomenal time at the event. We took pictures, watched the Vidal Sassoon movie, and heard a phenomenal speech from Vidal

Sassoon. Sassoon made a statement about becoming an innovator, and I could not stop crying. I felt like he was speaking directly to me.

The next day, I needed to shop for tools for my business. I was about to graduate, and I wanted to make sure I was prepared for the real world. I left that evening with tons of tools and products and needed to go back to the hotel to organize my items. As I was organizing, the light went off. I asked my friend to turn the light back on. She told me she was tired and needed to sleep. I remember feeling so angry. I turned the light back on and finished packing, we went back and forth. My friend took an earlier flight home the next day.

I was hard on myself for how I had reacted. I dropped down on my knees to pray.

"I need you to do something big in my life Lord. Please help me," I asked.

I decided not to allow the situation with my friend to keep me down, so I went to the last day of the event. As I walked in the door, I prayed for direction. When I looked up, I was standing in front of a celebrity/student panel. Students could ask celebrities questions. I raised my hand and a young lady came over to me. She asked my name and passed me the microphone to ask my question to the panel.

My question was, "How can a single mom of five children continue her education when classes are close to one thousand dollars a class?" No one knew how to respond, at first. The panel answered the best they knew how. Shortly afterwards, my name was called, and I was told that I would receive a seven-day training with Nick Arrojo. Before I had left Las Vegas for Chicago, I called Nick Arrojo's studio to ask if they had any scholarships available.

The lady who answered the phone told me they didn't offer scholarships. Once the panel discussion was over, a few of us gathered together. I remember throwing my hands up in the air.

"One year ago I was homeless and today I am exactly where I want to be," I said, tears flowing down my face.

The lady who had the microphone told me she would get back with me within thirty days. I went back home and continued to work hard; I only had a month until graduation.

I sat in class one day, and the instructor who didn't care for me asked for the people who were graduating that week to raise their hands. I did not raise my hand because I didn't want to get sent home for any reason. I was graduating that weekend.

Saturday morning came. I wore a khaki dress and knee length socks for my graduation. We normally wear uniforms. The instructor asked me why I wasn't in uniform.

I replied,

"Today is the day I can clock out and never return," I said. That was the most liberating feeling.

Before I left school the day of my graduation, I was called into the office by and asked if I could speak at my graduation. I said, "Yes."

Although I graduated and was finished with my hours and didn't need to go to school anymore the school had a date set up for anyone graduating in a certain period of time, to walk across the stage together. I was asked to speak at my formal graduation, in my cap and gown.

I was the first student to graduate from my class, because my hours were completed. I was never late or absent. I kept the commitment I made to myself when I enrolled in cosmetology school, and it paid off.

Once I got home, there were flowers waiting for me from the WELLA team. I received a call from Samantha Sirens, the lady who said she would call within thirty days. Samantha told me they were having an event in Las Vegas in July, if I wanted to attend. I went to the event and learned so much. She became my mentor, and her team helped me out a lot as well, including one very special person who is no longer with us. He showed me true passion in the industry.

During this time, I met an elderly lady who became my adopted grandmother. She kept my children for me as I traveled. My mentor spent the rest of the year exposing me to education. My family was adopted by the WELLA team for Christmas and gifts from all over the world came to my doorstep for my children. A color consultant position was available, and I got the job. What I loved the most about that season of my life was how much love strangers showed me and my family with no expectations. I am truly thankful for each of them. They taught me that my past didn't define me, my present didn't limit me, and my future had so much in store for me.

Chapter Seven

Excessive Truss Wrapped Around my Frock

I had a clothing collection called "Amikad" which is my name spelled backwards. The collection was sold at the mall and a boutique. I had a business partner who stood right by my side. We were very close, she taught me how to have patience. We ate breakfast together almost every morning. We were at our sewing machines daily designing clothes. We gave fashion shows to get the collection's name out to the public.

We made one huge mistake, and that was when a loan offer was mailed to my business partner. She asked me what I thought about it. I told her that I knew I couldn't pay the money back, so I didn't know if it was a good idea. We were both under the impression that we could make the money from the fashion show. She took the loan, we didn't make the money anticipated. She was stuck with the loan. Although, I told her I didn't have money to pay back once I get a little extra, I will give her money towards that loan.

I met with a salon owner, Bethel Washington in Las Vegas who wanted to sell her salon. If I knew what I know now, I would have never taken over the salon. It was in an old building, and the place needed tons of repairs. I invested money for repairs and remodeling that I made from servicing my clients to get the salon up to code. I handled the business deal totally backwards. I should've paid off the balance of the deposit and then remodeled. I wanted my clients to feel comfortable when they came through the door.

Here I was years later and stuck in another bad business decision. It was time for me to renew my contract, and I didn't have the balance owed. I had a meeting with Bethel and I asked for more time, but I was denied.

The locks were changed the next day and Bethel wouldn't let me in. I had tools inside. I went back again the follow day, she called the police. When the police came out, they told me I couldn't take anything out of the building.

The police said, "Your contract expired yesterday, you'll have to go to small claims court to obtain any equipment inside.

The salon was beautiful. I may have left with nothing but a learning experience. I was tired of fighting and I had already spoken to another salon owner who had a chair available for me. A few days later. Bethel gave me my tools.

During this transition with my career, my prayer life wasn't as strong as it normally would've been. I made a tremendous amount of decisions for my business, children, and lifestyle without seeking God first. I was all over the place with my decision making. I didn't realize how much my family was be affected by my behaviors.

At the time, my oldest daughter was entering her senior year of high school. She was a great student, and she played on the varsity basketball team. She had several collegiate coaches were scouting her, and her coaches were very supportive. I showed her my support financially, but I wish I was more visible and listened to what she was needed from me emotionally as a mother. She was obligated to help raise her four siblings due to my circumstance.

My son was in his junior year in high school, with the fluctuation of grades and many challenges. He played both varsity basketball and varsity volleyball. During that period in his life I wish I was more attentive to his needs. I continued to encourage him to complete school because he didn't get up on time for school, he hung out away from home several days at a time. I communicated my experiences in school with him, and how I wish I had someone pushing me through to graduation. I couldn't give up on him, and he graduated the following year.

My third son was a freshman in high school. He had good grades, and his teachers sent me emails about his phenomenal behavior. He played both volleyball and basketball. He was always very tender, caring, and loving. He was my number one fan. I wish I would've been more attentive and visible for him. I could look into his eyes and see that he needed me. He was slowly starting to follow his brother footsteps.

My fourth child was in the eighth grade. She had good grades and was a passionate cheerleader. At that age, she already demonstrated persistence and strong opinions. She was a mini me, very defiant and determined. We clashed so strong because she was going to do what she wanted to do. I wish I could've listened to her and given her more attention. I needed to be the person she could express herself with about anything.

My youngest child was in the sixth grade in elementary school. She struggled in class and with her grades. She played on her school's basketball team as well. She was very quiet, emotional, and the hugger in our family. She was our lovable butterfly. We were all going to counseling as a family, so we could talk about how we felt about the divorce, the transition, and how much my past was affecting me. I wish that she would've had a chance to have me around more than I was able to be. She was my child who taught me how to show love again.

That was a very interesting year. I realized how much I needed God, life seemed to be improving, but obstacles were more prevalent. I was improving with materialistic things, moved into a bigger home and got a new car. My prayer life wasn't the same a before and my relationship with God was struggling. I lost the peace of God that I once had.

My children were beginning to change into people I didn't know. They weren't respectful toward me or followed the house rules. I worked out regularly to relieve stress. I dropped down on my knees asking God to please help me and show me how to return to him. Life is so much better with God being my source. I experienced life both ways, and I choose God.

Once my oldest two children graduated, I felt like I was going to have a nervous breakdown and my blood pressure wouldn't stay down. I called my children's father, asked if my three younger children could go with him for the summer and possibly a school year. He said, " Absolutely my kids can come wherever I am." I bought their tickets. When I told them that I had tickets for them to go visit their dad in June, they weren't so happy. This shocked me because they always told me what their dad would do for them. Once we sat down to discuss the plans they were fine with it.

Chapter Eight
My Children's Point of View

I have talked about my children in the previous chapters, now you are going to hear the point of views about what life was like growing up.

My oldest daughter in her own words: Growing up without a dad was challenging yet so wonderful. My mom found joy in everything and kept us busy by taking us on walks, writing songs for us to sing, and taking us to amusement parks and water parks.

There were also times we had no clue what we were going to eat and my mom would get us all McChicken sandwiches from McDonald's. She sometimes would go without eating just so we could eat. I honestly think she thought I wouldn't notice.

There were nights I'd see her crying her eyes out. I would lay there and cry with her because I wanted to understand what was wrong. I couldn't understand until I experienced my first heartbreaking moment and everything she ever said made sense. From then on, I wanted to help her and be there for her as much as she was for me.

In a way, I felt heartbroken for my mom and for myself because I loved my dad, and I always will. I just knew there was a reason behind it all, even if I didn't understand it all at the time. Once I began to understand, I stopped being angry at my mom and our relationship got better.

Life with my parents together started off great based on what I remember and all the pictures I have seen. We had nice things and birthday parties together because of our close birthdays. We had Elmo costume characters come to our parties and enjoyed popcorn and cotton candy machines. We received gifts and money. We rode to the parties in limousines while wearing mink coats. It was amazing, and we were blessed.

I also remember going to multiple elementary schools and having to make new friends all the time due to our frequent moves. Through those experiences, I learned how to be social and how deal with different people. Moving helped me view the world in a new way, and I didn't truly understand what that meant until I got older.

I excelled in sports and my parents attended my games. I played on girls teams, boys teams, and even coed teams. I was involved in basketball, swimming, gymnastics, figure skating, cheerleading, and tennis for a little while. I grew to appreciate all sports, and I fell in love with basketball, which took my attention away from what was really going on. So even though I saw I didn't experience as much as often as my younger siblings who were too young to be anywhere but home.

I think my mom tried to teach me how to go down a better path than she did and how to be responsible early on in my life. Even though I didn't always listen, she continued to teach me. She also wanted me to avoid unnecessary obstacles by showing me where to go. Now, I am able to see everything she does as her way of loving me and trying to protect my siblings and me.

I think my mom is so many things. She's strong, beautiful, blessed, and motivated. She has such a kind heart but she knows when to be firm. I am honestly so proud of her progress — where she has come and where she is going. I can't wait to see what God has in store for my mom! I love you so much, mom. You are amazing, and I wouldn't trade you for the world! Teirra Hicks

My oldest son in his own words:

Life with my parents together seemed to me as our happiest time as an entire family. I initially thought that if our parents had stayed together we'd be more secure. Being the second oldest out of five kids, I started to become more aware of my parent's arguments. As the fights seemed to get worse, I became nervous, but tried to remain a kid.

When my mom officially moved us out to Las Vegas, it was a sad moment for me being the oldest boy. Once I saw my dad didn't even care to come say goodbye or fight for us, my entire perspective on the situation changed. It made me angry. The moving part wasn't scary for me because I was used to moving. Plus, we had constantly changed schools. In Las Vegas, we only attended two schools, which shows how hard my mom worked to raise us on her own. She took the time, even when she had none; she put the extra effort, even when she had no energy.

My mom wanted to teach us to be our best selves. My siblings and I had dramatically varied characters, but she wanted us all to know that we were God's children. She instilled in us the scriptural truth that if we kept our faith and believed in God, we could do all things through Christ who strengthened us. Another favorite was that God has not given us a spirit of fear but of power, love and, a sound mind. If I had to choose the most important truth I learned from my mom, it was not to fear.

My childhood was rough at points, but for the most part fun. I certainly feel I was forced to grow up a lot faster than a normal kid, even though at the time I thought my life was pretty normal. Having four siblings is an upper and a downer. You never get anything to yourself but you're never bored. I love each and every one of my siblings unconditionally. They made my childhood.

Honestly, my mom is my hero. She is the reason we came here to earth. She's the reason I am where I am today. She's such a positive icon. During all the problems I put her through, she never gave me the impression that she's done with me. My mom is by far the most influential person in my life. She looked challenges straight in the eyes and made a lot out of her life. My mom is virtuous in my eyes and by far, my favorite person. Terrell Hicks Jr.

My third child (son) in his own words:

My earliest memories of life with my parents together were amazing. I remember being homeschooled for a short time. My dad would be at work and my mom would provide homework for my younger sister and my older brother. We had a basketball hoop outside, and for recess, we would each get about 30 minutes to play. I also remember the times where they would both come to my games. There was no better feeling than having two parents show up to your game to support you. I'd say we were a pretty happy, loving family with a big house.

Then, I started to notice changes. I was in first grade when my teacher asked the class to raise our hands if our parents were still together. I happily raised my hand. Right after that week of school, my parents were arguing a lot and ended up being separated. I was staying at my mom's friend's house and my siblings, and I would see my dad every Wednesday evening to do something fun. Eventually they got back together but it wasn't the same.

My mom finally decided she no longer could be with my dad, and she took all of us to Las Vegas where we would start a new life. That is when I started to feel how life was without my dad. I felt left out because all of the other kids had dads to go home to, and I knew I couldn't come home to my dad. Although we would talk on the phone, it wasn't the same as being with him. When he was around, I used to wake up in the middle of the night and find my dad playing the Play Station. He would always make me cereal or ice cream with warm apple pie and let me watch or play with him. I no longer had that. I also didn't have him around to teach me basketball or how to be a man. That is what I missed the most.

Overall, I think my mother tried to teach me how to treat a woman when I am older as well as how to be polite and kind to everyone. But most of all, she wanted me to be a leader. She saw things in me that I didn't always see in myself. She wanted me to realize that with God anything is possible.

I think I had a pretty good childhood, although it was different. I have experienced some crazy things but it made me who I am today. Although I may have disagreed with some of the decisions my parents made, I still want to thank them both for the sacrifices they made for me and my siblings growing up, especially my mom. I think my mom is the hardest-working person I have ever met. I also think that she is extremely kind, loving, funny, goofy, honest, trustworthy, stylish, and professional.

I have the utmost respect for my mom, and I love her with all of my heart. I know that if she puts her mind to something, she is going to get it done regardless of how hard it may be to accomplish. My mother is very beautiful and has many gifts. My mom has been through a lot in her life, but she demonstrates joy.

Finally, my mother is my best friend. She is very easy to talk to, and I feel comfortable telling her anything. She likes to fit in with the new generation's dance moves and is good that them. She loves my siblings and me unconditionally and would do anything for us. Tyre Hicks

My fourth child (daughter) in her own words:

Growing up with my parents was amazing. We were always doing family activities together and money was never an issue, at least that I could tell. We lived in such beautiful homes, and the schools I attended were top notch. Having a big family was something I enjoyed more than anything else in this world. My sisters and I would go to gymnastics every weekend, while my dad would take my brothers bowling. I had such a good life.

Once my parents got divorced, and we relocated to Las Vegas things went downhill. I didn't care about moving, but our new living conditions were far from my favorite. Even though, I had always been a daddy's girl, living without him didn't have that much of an effect on my life. I think it was because I had my mom and all of my siblings around me.

My mom always taught us to be respectful, well-behaved kids. She also taught us that lying wouldn't get us anywhere and life because the truth would eventually come to light. The main thing she taught us was having a personal relationship with God. God has always been her number one source for everything, and she made sure to raise us on that path. We prayed as a family together every single night and prayer was a part of our daily routine.

Looking back at my childhood, I never realized how lucky I was. Even after moving to Las Vegas and struggling until my mom was able to get on her feet, we were so blessed. I can remember walking downstairs on Christmas morning with gifts from the front door all the way through the living room.

My mom is a very unique woman who loves her children, friends, and family more than anyone could love anything. She unlike any other person in this world and that's what makes her who she is. Even we she didn't have much, she would take her last just to put a smile on someone else's face. My mom has always been one to smile through the struggle. Even during worst moments of her life, she comes back with a smile on her face, brighter and stronger than before.

My mom and I are very much alike, and she wouldn't hesitate to tell you that herself. Even when I am upset with her, it only takes a few moments for me to remember how much she has sacrificed for my life and the love she shows me every day.

The cherry on top of this all is my mom's sense of fashion. From her hair, to her heels, to her green lipstick. My mom is an amazing woman. You have truly been blessed if you have ever gotten a chance to meet her. Tianna Hicks

My fifth child (daughter) in her own words:

When my parents were together, I was younger. They divorced before I was five years old. I can remember some of the little things, like my childhood home. I never really saw my parents arguing. When they did separate, I was too young to understand why. I did overhear some things that were said about the situation by my older siblings. Because I was the youngest of my siblings, they made sure to be careful about some of the things they said.

When we moved to Las Vegas, it was already obvious that my parents' relationship was over. Even though my mom and dad split up, I still loved them both the same. Growing up without my dad was especially hard. It's not like he wasn't there; he was there but just not in person. He always wanted his kids to know that he cared about each and every one of us, no matter what happened with him and my mom.

My mom always encouraged her kids to graduate and be successful — to do something with our lives. I think my mom tried to teach us how to be responsible and independent and to strive for greatness.

I loved my childhood because it was fun. We had a really close family, and we still love each other so much. Have you ever watched those movies about families that go to their grandparents' house and have a really big family reunion over the holidays? Imagine that, and that's what my family looks like on a holiday.

I think my mom is one of the most intelligent people I have ever met. My mom is inspired and kind. I think of my mom as a motivational speaker. If you're having a horrible day, my mom is a great person to talk and to ask for advice. Takyra Hicks

Chapter Nine

Exaggerated Array with Exclusive Remnants

I turned forty years old, and there were so many changes taking place in my life. For the first time in twenty years, I thought of myself. I gave myself a pretty-in-pink fortieth birthday party and invited everyone I could think of. I turned my car back into the dealership, sold everything in my house, and went to Africa.

My party was a great success; so many people came from different states to celebrate with me A breath of fresh air was well overdue, and I needed to make my own decisions regardless of what people thought of me. I prayed and trusted God and my instincts during this period of my life. Many people disagreed with my decision, just like they did when I left Detroit for Las Vegas.

People close to me besmirched my character behind my back. I had to determine if I was going to live the life they wanted me to live or live my own kind of life. Don't get me wrong, I was apprehensive, but I decided to live in that moment, dead or alive. I asked people to remember me as living to the fullest, if anything happened to me while I was in Africa.

So many years of my life, I lived for other people. I took care of others before myself and second-guessed myself too many times. But I would not do that anymore because I was born to be me. I decided not to focus on my weaknesses and instead to embrace my strengths. I began to understand the meaning of setting boundaries at age thirty-five. I didn't understand my self-worth until I was forty years old. I actually have come to realize that I can't love you without loving me; I can't help you before I help myself; and the love I share with you is a gift.

So now, I have a different approach to everything that I do. I no longer need validation from others. However, I do enjoy learning and growing with others and making my own final decisions. I have embraced a freedom that I never knew existed within me, a power invested in me through God. Everyone has that gift, and whether or not we use it, is our choice.

Africa gave me a different outlook at life, in many different ways. I lived as an African queen with many people in the community serving, cooking, and cleaning for me. This was extremely different for me because in the United States, I took care of so many. So much of what we had in the U.S. was available there: movies, ice cream shops, and fast food restaurants like Kentucky Fried Chicken. My favorite place was a store that sold meat pies, and I frequently bought the corn and pears sold on the corner.

The electricity could go off at any time, and there was no middle class. Yet, people were happy with what they had. Going to the market was like going to a flea market in Detroit. I traveled to Benin City, Lagos, Ekpoma, and I lived in Abuja. I traveled to Detroit every three months to make sure that my children had everything that they needed. I attended their basketball games to give them moral support.

I learned how to appreciate life while I was in Africa. I was so fortunate to have the opportunity to see the Motherland for myself. I had so much more to be thankful for in the United States. I really began to examine myself and how I wanted to make a difference in my family once I returned home.

Leaving everything behind made me appreciate what I had more than before. I also realized that a lot of my children's behaviors stemmed from my own. They needed my love and attention, and I didn't know how to give it to them because I needed love and attention. I was deprived my whole life, so how could I give to someone else what I didn't totally understand?

What I thought was love, was control. I was controlling in my marriage, with my children, and with anyone else close to me. I blamed everyone else and always wanted to be right. Now, I take full responsibility for my life. I seek to create an atmosphere of love by learning what it means to love and to receive love.

Whether I am wrong or right, being myself from within is what's important to me. I no longer want to reflect my childhood and am releasing the person that I was born to be in this universe. I am loving, kind, giving, fair, wise, and a great person to get to know. I am a ride-or-die friend, a hard-working mother, and an imperfect individual, who asks for forgiveness from anyone who I have hurt, disappointed, and caused to stumble. I also forgive others who have hurt me in the past — from the deepest roots of pain to the slightest thought, I forgive you! Love is what makes the world go around.

Chapter Ten

Elegant Array with Rectified Ridges

After my third visit to Detroit from Africa, I decided to stay. I got a job, moved into a condo, and took my kids to school as often as possible. They stayed with me on the weekends and sometimes during the week. I sat my children down and told them that I was going to go back to Las Vegas, so that I could prepare to get them a few months later.

I quit my job and drove back to Las Vegas. I found a job at a salon through a mutual friend. I asked the salon owner if I could sleep in her salon at night; she approved. I drove around during the day and either slept at the salon, a hotel, or a friend's house. I started going to the park in the mornings and listened to Charles Stanley daily.

I received a call from my cousin asking if my youngest son could spend his senior year with them in Portland, Oregon. I actually felt like it was a great opportunity for him but supported his decision either way. My cousin started getting my boys every summer, two years after my family relocated to Las Vegas. My youngest son decided he wanted to go back!

While he flew to Portland, I flew to Detroit to pick up my girls. I still hadn't found a place to live, so we stayed in a hotel. I knew that I needed to find a place before school started.

While my girls and I were in California to see my youngest son in a basketball tournament, we met two ladies who had flown in from Portland to watch my son play. I thought that was amazing because they barely knew him. I also met other team parents.

I mentioned to one of the parents that I was looking for a place in Portland because I couldn't find anything in Las Vegas. She told me that she and her husband owned apartments in Portland and asked if I wanted to look into them. I immediately told her that my credit was bad. She still gave me the information, and even though I was denied by the apartment manager, the owners approved me. I was in tears, and I couldn't believe what I was hearing.

I scheduled an appointment to fly in so that I could do a walk through and make a down payment. I also scheduled an interview at a salon. I got the job and my apartment.

Once I moved there, I went looking for food pantries throughout the city. I was able to sign up for "Dress for Success," a program that helps ladies improve their lives. I found another program that helped me with budgeting and time management. I was even able to furnish my home for free.

My work start date was pushed back because I failed the first cosmetology license test. I passed the second time around. I worked at the first salon for three months and then moved to a different salon, which I love. It's been two years since I've been in

Portland. I am back in school for fashion design, and one day my garments will be all around the world.

The Pretty Floral Dress

This chapter in my life relies totally on God for direction, as I walk in faith to complete each task. I am improving my parenting skills, enhancing my career skills, and remembering self-care. I am creating an atmosphere of love, peace, and happiness from within through my father from above where ever I go.

God turned my pain into rose petals, and now I am wearing the roses. I will make the best of life with all the imperfections that's to come. I am not defined by my mistakes or my past, I am redeemed by the love of the Lord.

For every child, teenager, or adult that just read my book, it starts with a mindset, owning who you are, good or bad. Take a few minutes to meditate in silence with a prayer, or thoughts of positivity. Create a plan, make the required adjustments in your life to meet your goals financially, emotionally, or physically. Follow through and be intentional about your life.

Don't allow your childhood to define you, your mistakes to control you, or your decisions to limit you. You belong, I believe in you and the world needs you.

I've learned through it all, in order for me to give any part of me, I must take from a place that isn't causing me regret. It's imperative for me to pay attention to my motives. As I set boundaries and treat people like I desire to be treated, I will never have it all together. I can only control me.